PATRICK MAHOMES

NFL SENSATION

BY JAMES MONSON

Essential Library

An Imprint of Abdo Publishing
abdobooks.com

ABDOBOOKS.COM

Published by Abdo Publishing, a division of ABDO, PO Box 398166, Minneapolis, Minnesota 55439. Copyright © 2020 by Abdo Consulting Group, Inc. International copyrights reserved in all countries. No part of this book may be reproduced in any form without written permission from the publisher. Essential Library™ is a trademark and logo of Abdo Publishing.

Printed in the United States of America, North Mankato, Minnesota.
042019
092019

Cover Photo: Charlie Riedel/AP Images
Interior Photos: Kevin Terrell/AP Images, 4, 8; Kelvin Kuo/AP Images, 7, 13, 71; Victor Texcucano/Tyler Morning Telegraph/AP Images, 14, 20; Kathy Willens/AP Images, 17; Jamie Lamor Thompson/Shutterstock Images, 22; Mo Khursheed/TFV Media/AP Images, 24; Tori Eichberger/Zach Long/Lubbock Avalanche-Journal/ AP Images, 27; Jerod Foster/Icon Sportswire/AP Images, 29; Tim Warner/Cal Sport Media/AP Images, 32; Zackary Brame/Icon Sportswire/AP Images, 35; Ken Murray/Icon Sportswire/AP Images, 37; Jacob Snow/Icon Sportswire/AP Images, 38; Sam Grenadier/Icon Sportswire/AP Images, 42; Andrew Dieb/Icon Sportswire/ AP Images, 44; David J. Phillip/AP Images, 48; Mark Rogers/Lubbock Avalanche- Journal/AP Images, 51; Chelsea Purgahn/Tyler Morning Telegraph/AP Images, 54; Ed Zurga/AP Images, 57, 76, 79; John Leyba/Denver Post/AP Images, 59; Orlin Wagner/AP Images, 60; Paul Abell/AP Images, 63; Gene J. Puskar/AP Images, 64; Michael Dwyer/AP Images, 69; Reed Hoffmann/AP Images, 74; Elise Amendola/AP Images, 82; Perry Knotts/AP Images, 85; Greg Trott/AP Images, 86; Jeff Roberson/ AP Images, 88; David Tulis/UPI/Newscom, 90; Doug Benc/Old Spice/AP Images, 94; Colin E. Braley/Dixie Ultra®/AP Images, 97

Editor: Patrick Donnelly
Series Designer: Laura Graphenteen

LIBRARY OF CONGRESS CONTROL NUMBER: 2018967348

PUBLISHER'S CATALOGING-IN-PUBLICATION DATA
Names: Monson, James, author.
Title: Patrick Mahomes: NFL sensation / by James Monson
Other title: NFL sensation
Description: Minneapolis, Minnesota: Abdo Publishing, 2020 | Series: Star athletes |
        Includes online resources and index.
Identifiers: ISBN 9781532119897 (lib. bdg.) | ISBN 9781532174728 (ebook) | ISBN
        9781644940969 (pbk.)
Subjects: LCSH: Quarterbacks (Football)--United States--Biography--Juvenile literature.
        | Football players--United States--Biography--Juvenile literature. | Kansas
        City Chiefs (Football team)--Juvenile literature. | Sports--Biography--Juvenile
        literature.
Classification: DDC 796.3326409 [B]--dc23

CONTENTS

PATIENCE
REWARDED

When Patrick Mahomes took the field for the Kansas City Chiefs on September 9, 2018, it was a landmark moment. Though it wasn't his first game with the Chiefs, this day was special.

The Chiefs had selected Mahomes in the first round of the 2017 National Football League (NFL) Draft. But he spent his rookie season on the bench, watching and learning and preparing for this day. When Kansas City traded starting quarterback Alex Smith in the off-season, it signaled that the team was ready for Mahomes to take over.

His first test came on the road against the Los Angeles Chargers. The Chargers were a division rival that just missed the playoffs in 2017. Behind veteran quarterback Philip Rivers, the Chargers could put up lots of points on offense. Pro Bowl players Casey Hayward in the defensive backfield and Joey Bosa on the line led a tough defense.

Patrick Mahomes made his 2018 debut against the Chargers in Los Angeles.

It wouldn't be an easy opening game for Kansas City and its young quarterback.

But the Chiefs had one thing in their favor. They were the visiting team, but this was no typical road game. As Mahomes and his teammates entered the StubHub Center in Los Angeles, the players felt right at home. The Chargers were playing only their second year in Los Angeles after moving from San Diego. The team hadn't yet built much fan support. This allowed opposing fans the chance to buy tickets. Thousands of people wearing red and white—the Chiefs' colors—came to the game. They were ready to cheer on Kansas City and see what Mahomes could do as the team's new starting quarterback.

NOT A FIRST IMPRESSION

Before taking the field against the Chargers in September 2018, Mahomes had a chance to experience NFL regular-season action in 2017. With Kansas City already qualified for the playoffs, the Chiefs let then starter Alex Smith rest, allowing Mahomes to get the start against the Denver Broncos. Kansas City won the December game 27–24 as Mahomes threw for 284 yards.

GETTING STARTED

However, those fans would have to wait. The Chiefs kicked off to start the game. When the defense stopped the Chargers to force a punt, it appeared Mahomes's time had come. Then Kansas City's Tyreek Hill returned the punt 91 yards for a touchdown, forcing Mahomes

Mahomes used his feet in the first quarter to help the Chiefs get a first down.

to wait even longer. By the time he finally took the field with 9:20 left in the first quarter, it was already 7–3 Chiefs.

Mahomes entered the game to a large cheer from the Chiefs fans. It didn't take long for him to show why he was a top-10 draft pick. On his third play, the Chiefs faced third-and-short. Mahomes dropped back to pass,

needing three yards for a first down to keep the drive going. He searched for an open receiver, but the Chargers had them all covered. That's when Mahomes realized his best chance to make the first down was to run. He tucked the ball under his arm and found a hole on the right side of the field. He ran through and was tackled just past the first-down marker.

Mahomes's quick thinking and speed are a big part of what makes him an excellent quarterback. He was about to show off another one of his most important assets: his accurate arm. Two plays after he scrambled for the first down, Mahomes faked a handoff and dropped back to pass. With a defender running toward him at full speed, Mahomes threw the ball quickly to Hill. The ball went to a spot where only Hill could catch it, showing Mahomes's accuracy as a passer. The Kansas City wide receiver caught the ball in stride about 10 yards downfield and took off sprinting toward the far sideline. The Los Angeles defenders couldn't catch him. Soon, Hill was running full speed with nothing but grass in front of him. Hill's second touchdown of the day was Mahomes's first NFL touchdown pass. It would be the first of many.

Chiefs head coach Andy Reid goes over strategy with Mahomes during the Chargers game.

TERRIFIC TYREEK

A strong cast of teammates helped Patrick Mahomes thrive from day one. At the top of that list was wide receiver Tyreek Hill. Against the Chargers, Mahomes completed seven passes to Hill for 169 yards and two touchdowns. That success continued week after week in 2018.

On the last play of the first quarter, Mahomes showed off another of his valuable skills: arm strength. He lofted a pass 30 yards downfield to Hill, who had three defenders closing in on him. The receiver rewarded Mahomes with an acrobatic catch. Less than halfway into his first start, Mahomes had established a special connection with Hill, the team's top receiver.

STAYING HOT

In the second half, Hill continued to play a big role. He thrived in both the Chiefs' running game and passing games. On the Chiefs' first drive after halftime, Mahomes's pass to receiver Sammy Watkins put the ball inside the Los Angeles 5-yard line. Mahomes flipped the ball to De'Anthony Thomas, who ran the ball into the end zone for a touchdown. It was a simple pitch to Thomas, who was running through the Chiefs' backfield just behind the offensive linemen. But it also counted as another touchdown pass for Mahomes.

Now leading 24–12, the Chiefs began pulling away. An interception gave Kansas City the ball back deep in its own territory. On third down with 13 yards to go, Mahomes scrambled to find room to throw. Finally, with his front foot in the air and all of his weight on his back foot, Mahomes threw a pass that darted through the air to Hill. The five-foot-ten-inch (1.8 m) receiver dove to the ground to make the catch near midfield to get the first down.

A few plays later, Mahomes was back to pass once again. The Chiefs were now inside the Chargers' 40-yard line. With the offensive line keeping the defense away from Mahomes, he stood without any pressure and waited for a receiver to get open. Finally, he lofted a pass down the sideline. A Los Angeles defender leaped as if he had a chance to catch the ball. But it landed right in the arms of fullback Anthony Sherman. His only catch of the day was a big one as he rumbled into the end zone for another Chiefs score.

With Kansas City leading 31–20 in the fourth quarter, the Chiefs recovered a fumble inside the Los Angeles 5-yard line. Soon after, Mahomes found Hill once again. The speedy Kansas City receiver took another pitch behind the line of scrimmage and cruised into the end zone. That gave Kansas City a 38–20 lead.

EXCEEDING EXPECTATIONS

The Chiefs believed in Mahomes, but not everybody believed in the Chiefs. *Sports Illustrated*, for example, predicted that Kansas City would finish the season with a 7–9 record.[1] But after his four-touchdown performance in the season opener, Mahomes grabbed the attention of other NFL players, who recognized his skills.

"Andy Reid finally bought the Ferrari his offense needed."[2]
— Will Brinson, CBS Sports writer, on the Chiefs improving because of Mahomes's arrival

Los Angeles scored one more time to make the final score 38–28. With four touchdowns and more than 250 passing yards, Mahomes had a successful debut as the Chiefs' starting quarterback. Just as importantly, he had shown the unique abilities that the team hoped would lead to great success. He could pass the ball long and on target. He could make plays with his feet. And when a play broke down, Mahomes didn't lose his cool. Instead, he seemed to always find a way to make something happen. Mahomes was on his way to becoming a big-time star.

Mahomes is congratulated by Chargers quarterback Philip Rivers after the Chiefs' victory.

FOLLOWING IN DAD'S FOOTSTEPS

Patrick Lavon Mahomes II was born on September 17, 1995, in Tyler, Texas. He was named after his father, Pat Mahomes. His mother is Randi Martin. He has a younger brother, Jackson, and sister, Mia.

Patrick, who goes by his full name to differentiate himself from his father, shared his dad's passion for sports. The older Mahomes was a pitcher who reached the major leagues. Pat Mahomes's career shaped much of Patrick's early life. The entire family moved wherever Pat was playing. As a result, Patrick lived for a time in Minnesota, Massachusetts, and New York. During that time, Patrick often went to the ballpark with his father and watched the players prepare up close.

Patrick Mahomes makes a play at quarterback for Whitehouse High School in Whitehouse, Texas, in 2013.

FATHER AND SON

Pat Mahomes made his major league debut in 1992 at age 21. He pitched in the major leagues for 11 years and in Japan for two seasons. After playing multiple years in independent baseball leagues, Pat retired from baseball in 2009. He now spends much of his time traveling around the country to watch his son play football.

The Minnesota Twins drafted Pat in the sixth round of the 1988 Major League Baseball (MLB) Draft. He worked his way up through the Twins' minor league system. In 1992, he made his MLB debut. After more than four years with the Twins, Pat bounced between the Boston Red Sox, New York Mets, Texas Rangers, Chicago Cubs, and Pittsburgh Pirates. His last year in the majors was 2003.

In 2000, Pat and the Mets won the National League (NL) pennant, setting up a World Series showdown against the New York Yankees. Just five years old, Patrick had an up-close view of life in baseball's biggest spotlight. Patrick wowed his father by catching the fly balls hit by the major league players during batting practice.

"When we were in the World Series, I would let him go out to center field with me and let him shag balls," Pat said. "The coaches were wary that he was going to get hit, but I told them if he gets hit one time, he will learn—then he won't do it again. As I was saying it, [teammate] Robin

Patrick and his father's New York Mets teammate Mike Hampton shag fly balls in batting practice during the 2000 World Series.

Ventura hit a ball out to left-center. . . . It was the first time he caught a fly ball off a big leaguer's bat."[1]

TAKING ROOT IN TEXAS

When he was young, Patrick's parents divorced. Pat and Randi remained close, and Patrick kept a good relationship with both parents. However, the family no longer followed

EARLY GUIDANCE

Patrick's godfather is former MLB reliever LaTroy Hawkins. Hawkins and Pat Mahomes became friends when they were both in the Minnesota Twins minor league system in the 1990s. The two stayed close for many years afterward. Hawkins always had a close eye on Patrick's development as an athlete and attended Patrick's first NFL start in 2018.

"As a little kid, you knew that Patrick was going to be an outstanding athlete," Hawkins said. "He could run, he could throw a baseball, throw a football, much easier than other kids his age."[2]

Pat wherever his career took him. Instead, Patrick settled with Randi in Tyler in 2001.

While parts of his life changed, Patrick remained committed to sports. He played multiple sports as a kid through his time at Whitehouse High School in neighboring Whitehouse, Texas. Though he thrived in basketball and football early on, he most loved baseball. Patrick played on the varsity baseball team for all four years of high school. At different times he took the field as pitcher, shortstop, and all three outfield positions. He once pitched a no-hitter and struck out 16 batters in the first game of a doubleheader. In the second game, Patrick played in the field and had three hits at the plate. That versatility led to his making the all-state team as a junior and senior. Scouts from professional teams often showed up to watch him play.

In basketball, Patrick also played at the varsity level all four years as a guard. As a senior, he was one of the team's leading scorers, averaging 19 points per game. In his final playoff run, Patrick combined for 86 points in two games and helped to bring his team to the state semifinals.

As Patrick grew older, his love for football increased. As a junior in high school, he took over as the starting quarterback for the Whitehouse varsity team. In just his second start, he threw for 500 yards and led his team to a 38–33 win.

"I think that's when it finally clicked for Patrick Mahomes, what it's like to be the quarterback of a football team," said Adam Cook, Patrick's offensive coordinator at Whitehouse. "There's nothing like it. He can be on the mound, and he can be the pitcher, or he can be the point guard in basketball, but there's nothing like being the quarterback of a football team."[3]

Many people around Patrick figured he would pursue baseball after high school. However, some college football programs took notice of him during his junior year. One of those programs was Texas Tech University. During a visit to the campus in Lubbock, Texas, in 2013, Patrick met

BROTHERLY LOVE

Growing up just four years apart, Patrick and Jackson were very competitive and had their fair share of fights. One resulted in a broken door. Both were good at sports, too. While Patrick was drawn more to football and baseball, Jackson found his passion on the basketball court. Now that they are adults, the two are close. They talk on the phone and text frequently.

Patrick poses with his father, brother, and mother after being named the 2013 Texas Associated Press Sports Editors football player of the year.

with the coaches. He announced during the trip he was planning on playing college football and baseball for the Red Raiders.

As a senior, Patrick led Whitehouse to the school's first district championship. The team finished with a 12–1 record. After passing for 4,619 yards, Patrick was named an all-state player as well as the Texas Associated Press Sports Editors football player of the year.

ALL-AMERICAN KID

As he thrived in sports, Patrick succeeded in other areas, too. His grades were strong enough that he was able to take college classes while in high school. He also met his girlfriend, Brittany Matthews, while in high school. Both came from Tyler and both were good athletes. While Patrick was making headlines in football and baseball, Brittany was a standout soccer player.

All of the success suggested Patrick might have a bright future in college football. However, Texas Tech was the only school from a major conference to offer him a scholarship. Different theories exist as to why Patrick failed to draw much interest. It's possible that college football coaches were wary of his commitment to the sport. During the football off-season, Patrick played basketball and baseball instead of working with a private quarterback coach or attending summer football camps, as many of the top high school quarterbacks around the country did.

DUAL SUCCESS STORIES

While Patrick was excelling on the field in high school, so was his girlfriend, Brittany Matthews. She was a good soccer player at Whitehouse High School. Later she went on to the University of Texas at Tyler. While playing Division III collegiate soccer, Matthews recorded the second-most goals in school history. She had a short professional career in Iceland before becoming a personal trainer.

Mahomes attends an event with girlfriend Brittany Matthews in February 2019.

Plus, Patrick was really good at baseball. College football coaches might have thought he would follow in his dad's footsteps and pursue a professional baseball career. They had good reason to think that. Even Texas Tech didn't know for sure that Patrick was coming.

Patrick graduated from high school in the spring of 2014. He had a decision to make. He knew he'd likely be selected in the MLB Draft. But he wasn't sure whether he wanted to play pro baseball. In talking with his parents, he decided that compensation could make his decision easier. If a team offered him a signing bonus of at least $2 million, he'd play baseball.

Going into the draft in June, experts predicted Patrick might be selected around the third or fourth round. When the draft came around, Patrick had to wait until the thirty-seventh round to hear his name called by the Detroit Tigers. Most players drafted after the tenth round receive a signing bonus of less than $100,000. This made Patrick's decision easy: he was off to Texas Tech.

A BALANCING ACT

Patrick Mahomes arrived on the Texas Tech campus in the summer of 2014. He spent his time preparing for his freshman year with the Red Raiders football team. When Mahomes committed to play for Texas Tech, he was still considered a work in progress. With that in mind, Mahomes wasn't expected to play as a freshman. Instead, the Red Raiders planned to bring back quarterbacks Baker Mayfield and Davis Webb. The two had split time in 2013. But Mayfield decided after the 2013 season to transfer to Oklahoma. That left Webb and Mahomes as the only quarterbacks on the Texas Tech roster.

Having played in ten games in 2013, Webb was still the presumed starter. Few freshmen, especially quarterbacks, see action right away for major programs. They need time to adapt to the much

Mahomes looks on from the bench during his freshman season at Texas Tech.

higher level of play. But Mahomes knew he should be ready to play just in case.

One advantage Mahomes had was his familiarity with the Red Raiders' offense. He joined a program known for its high-flying passing attack. He had played in a similarly up-tempo offense in high school.

Texas Tech headed into the 2014 season with reasonably high expectations after winning eight games the season prior. Both Webb and Red Raiders head coach Kliff Kingsbury were heading into their second seasons in Lubbock.

Webb started the season as quarterback. Mahomes watched from the sideline as Webb led the team to wins against Central Arkansas and the University of Texas–El Paso. In the third game, the Red Raiders lost to Arkansas at home 49–28. The fourth game was an important one. Texas Tech traveled to Oklahoma State for the Big 12 Conference opener. Once again, Mahomes watched from the sideline. However, in the fourth quarter, he got his opportunity.

TAKING ADVANTAGE

Webb left the game with an injured shoulder. The young freshman entered with his team trailing 35–28 in the

With an Oklahoma State player in his face, Mahomes throws his first touchdown pass as a college quarterback.

final quarter. On his first collegiate play, Mahomes faced a third down with 24 yards to go at his own 13-yard line. After taking the snap, Mahomes scrambled through the Oklahoma State defense for 14 yards. The Red Raiders had to punt, but it was a promising start for Mahomes.

Later in the game, the Red Raiders started to move the ball, though they trailed 45–28. After a few runs and defensive penalties on Oklahoma State, Texas Tech was approaching the end zone. With the ball at the 4-yard line, Mahomes dropped back to pass. He found receiver Jakeem Grant, who caught the ball for a touchdown. It was Mahomes's first touchdown pass as a college quarterback. He finished the game with 20 yards passing and 16 yards rushing. However, Texas Tech lost the game 45–35.

Following the loss, Webb returned to his position as the team's starter for the next four weeks. On October 25 in a game against Texas Christian University (TCU), Webb left the game with a leg injury. Mahomes came on in relief with his team trailing by more than 30 points. Mahomes threw a touchdown pass, but it proved to be inconsequential as TCU won 82–27.

Webb's injury forced him to miss the following game, which meant Mahomes earned his first collegiate start on November 1. It was a tough matchup against rival Texas. With the team 3–5 on the season, Mahomes had a chance to turn things around for Texas Tech. The Red Raiders led 6–3 early. However, a concussion forced Mahomes out

Mahomes is helped off the field after suffering a concussion against Texas in his first collegiate start.

of the game in the second quarter. He watched from the locker room as Texas Tech lost 34–13.

   After a loss to Oklahoma, Mahomes was 0–2 as a starter heading into a game at Iowa State. By the fourth quarter, Mahomes had thrown three touchdown passes, but Texas Tech trailed 31–27. The Red Raiders took over on the Iowa State side of the field with less than six minutes to play.

Mahomes faked a handoff and threw a short pass to running back Kenny Williams. With blockers in front of him, Williams broke free and ran 44 yards for a touchdown. Texas Tech led 34–31. The next time Mahomes had the ball, he took a knee to close out the game. He had his first win as a starter at Texas Tech.

FINISHING STRONG

The Red Raiders had one game remaining, and it was a big one. They were set to play Baylor at AT&T Stadium, home of the Dallas Cowboys. Baylor had one of the best teams in the country. That showed as the Bears went out and built a big lead. With his team down 45–20 late in the third quarter, Mahomes put on a show to remember.

"I think he just has that knack. Anytime we put him in, it's not always pretty, but he finds a way to move the ball down and put it in the end zone."[1]

— *Kliff Kingsbury, Texas Tech head coach, on Mahomes prior to his first collegiate start*

In the game's final 17 minutes, Mahomes threw four touchdown passes, each of them 40 yards or longer. With 1:42 to go in the game and Texas Tech down 48–40, Mahomes threw his sixth touchdown pass of the day, cutting Baylor's lead to 48–46. However, Texas Tech failed a two-point conversion to tie the game. The 48–46 score held.

FROM WHITEHOUSE TO TEXAS TECH

Mahomes did not attend one of the traditional Texas high school football powers. But he was part of a team that had some elite talent. One of his receivers, Dylan Cantrell, went on to join Mahomes at Texas Tech. Cantrell and Mahomes played together for three seasons. In their final season together at Texas Tech in 2016, Mahomes threw eight touchdown passes to Cantrell. The Los Angeles Chargers selected Cantrell in the sixth round of the 2018 NFL Draft.

But Mahomes had passed for 598 yards. At the time, it was the most passing yards in a single game for a freshman quarterback in the Big 12 Conference.

The Red Raiders finished the season 4–8 and did not qualify for a bowl game. It was a step back from the season before. Texas Tech especially struggled in Big 12 play, finishing with a 2–7 conference record.

Afterward, Mahomes turned his attention to the Red Raiders baseball team. However, his football commitment didn't go away. He had to balance the baseball season with the football team's spring practice. Mahomes missed baseball games to attend football practice. With the

Mahomes, left, and offensive lineman Alfredo Morales celebrate a Texas Tech touchdown against Baylor.

starting quarterback position up for grabs, he began to put more focus on football.

Going into the 2015 football season, Texas Tech wasn't expected to be much better than it was the previous season. The defense had allowed 34 or more points nine times in 2014 and had hired a new defensive coordinator to try to improve things. But that meant the defense would have to learn a new system.

Fans were more optimistic about the offense. Mahomes and Webb headed into the season competing for the starting quarterback job. Each had shown potential in 2014, as Texas Tech ranked fifth in the nation in passing yards per game.

PUTTING UP POINTS

Fans and even the coaches were torn as to which quarterback should start. Eventually, Mahomes got the nod. His first test was against Sam Houston State University, a small, nonconference opponent. Late in the first quarter, Mahomes stepped up and threw a long pass down the sideline. Receiver Devin Lauderdale caught it and ran in for a 64-yard touchdown. The long strike was similar to the ones Mahomes had thrown the season before. In total, he passed for 425 yards and four touchdown passes that day.

The next week, Mahomes ran for a pair of touchdowns in another winning effort. This time Tech beat the University of Texas–El Paso 69–20. He was now impressing fans with both his throws and running ability.

After helping his team to a 3–0 start, Mahomes's biggest test of the season came against third-ranked TCU. It was a hard-fought game. With less than eight minutes left, Texas Tech trailed 48–45. Mahomes and the Red Raiders' offense began a drive on their own 10-yard line. He quickly got to work.

In seven plays, Mahomes led the team to midfield. Then he threw a short pass to running back Justin Stockton along the sideline. Stockton avoided a tackle and sprinted down the field. He outran a pair of defenders and dove into the end zone for a 50-yard touchdown. The Red Raiders led 52–48 with just under six minutes left in the game.

However, that was still plenty of time for TCU, who scored another touchdown to go up 55–52. That left one last drive for Mahomes. He took the Red Raiders to midfield. With time running out, they had one last shot. Mahomes hit wide receiver DeAndre Washington, who

Mahomes throws a pass under heavy pressure from two TCU defenders.

then pitched it to a teammate. The Red Raiders passed the ball around twice more. Eventually, it ended up in the hands of wide receiver Jakeem Grant, who raced toward the end zone. But the TCU defenders pushed him out-of-bounds at the 10-yard line. The Red Raiders had fallen just short.

ADVICE FROM A PRO

Although Patrick Mahomes decided to pursue football, others thought his future was brighter in baseball. While Pat Mahomes was playing with the Texas Rangers in 2001, one of his teammates was star shortstop Alex Rodriguez. During that time, Patrick got to know Rodriguez, who gave his teammate's young son some advice.

"I said, 'Now listen to me, if you don't hear one thing that I ever tell you, you better listen to this. There is no money, there is no future, there is no history in football. You have to play baseball!'" Rodriguez recalled in 2018. "Well, he reminded me of that recently and, boy, am I glad he did not listen to me!"[2]

Mahomes started all 12 regular-season games as a sophomore. In the final game of the season, Texas Tech defeated Texas 48–45 to improve to 7–5. This was good enough to earn an invitation to the Texas Bowl in nearby Houston, where the Red Raiders lost to Louisiana State (LSU) 56–27. Despite the defeat, it was a positive year for Mahomes. He led the nation with 393 yards of total offense per game and was the youngest quarterback in National Collegiate Athletic Association (NCAA) history to total 5,000 yards passing and rushing in one season.

Shortly after the football season ended in January 2016, Mahomes made the decision to leave the Texas Tech baseball team. He wanted to devote all of his time to football.

"He loves the team atmosphere about it," Pat Mahomes said. "In baseball, if he's pitching, he could take over a game. If he had his good stuff, it's a good chance

LSU took down Mahomes in the Texas Bowl.

he was going to win the game. . . . But football is a game where you've got to have everybody playing well to be successful. I think he loves that. I think he loves being in a locker room with that many guys, all of them pulling for the same goal."[3]

GAINING
MOMENTUM

After two seasons at Texas Tech, Mahomes had established himself as a strong college quarterback. Webb, upon being moved to a backup role, transferred out of the program. This left no question as to who would lead the team in 2016. And with another strong showing during his junior year, some scouts thought he might even have a chance to skip his senior year and move up to the NFL.

Mahomes was able to pick up right where he left off the year before. In the season opener against Stephen F. Austin, Mahomes threw a 13-yard touchdown pass less than three minutes into the game. By the time the game was finished, Mahomes had thrown for 483 yards and four touchdowns. He also led the team with 57 rushing yards and two more touchdowns on the ground in a 69–17 win.

Mahomes started the 2016 season with a big game against Stephen F. Austin.

CLOSE WITH COACH

During Mahomes's time at Texas Tech, he spent a lot of time working with head coach Kliff Kingsbury. As a former Texas Tech quarterback himself, Kingsbury knew a thing or two about playing quarterback at a high level.

"He has the work ethic and he has the mind," Mahomes said of Kingsbury. "Whatever he does, I know he'll have success doing it."[1]

The offensive surge continued for Texas Tech in the early part of that season. In the second game of the season, Mahomes threw for 540 yards and five touchdowns at Arizona State. He put up similar numbers in the next two games. Texas Tech scored at least 50 points in each of its first four games. However, opponents also were scoring at will against the Tech defense. By the halfway point of the season, Texas Tech had a 3–3 record. The next game was a daunting one as the Red Raiders faced off against Oklahoma.

MEMORABLE SHOOT-OUT

Any conference game is important. The game on October 22 carried extra meaning for the Red Raiders, though. That's because the Sooners were led by star quarterback Baker Mayfield. He had begun his college career at Texas Tech and started as a freshman in 2013. However, after being told he'd have to compete for the starting job as a sophomore, Mayfield transferred to Oklahoma. This marked the first time Mayfield had played in Lubbock since transferring.

Mahomes had high expectations of his own. Oklahoma, ranked number 16 in the nation, is a traditional college football power. Plus, the game was being broadcast on national TV. Mahomes knew this was a great opportunity to show off his skills.

Early on, however, it was all about Mayfield. He threw two long touchdown passes in the first four minutes to give the Sooners a quick 13–0 lead. Texas Tech methodically worked its way back into the game. A touchdown run and field goal cut the score to 13–10. Oklahoma soon scored another touchdown. Again, the Red Raiders answered. Mahomes took the snap and darted 11 yards for his first touchdown of the day. It was now 20–17, Oklahoma.

The rest of the game followed the same pattern, with Oklahoma scoring to pad its lead and Texas Tech clawing back to make it close.

MUTUAL RESPECT

Though Mahomes and Mayfield were on opposite sides in their epic 2016 game, the two quarterbacks had respect for one another. Mayfield had hosted Mahomes on the latter's recruiting trip to Texas Tech. They got a chance to renew their friendly rivalry in the NFL in 2018, when Mahomes and the Chiefs visited Mayfield and the Cleveland Browns. That time, Mahomes came out on top with more passing yards (375 to 297) and touchdowns (three to two), and the Chiefs won 37–21.

Even Mahomes looked like he couldn't believe the numbers on the scoreboard when Texas Tech played Oklahoma in 2016.

As the game entered the fourth quarter, Mahomes used his legs once again on a 22-yard run to cut Oklahoma's lead to 51–45. With Mahomes and Mayfield leading their teams to touchdown drive after touchdown drive, the score increased rapidly. Every time Mayfield and Oklahoma scored to go back up by two touchdowns, Mahomes responded.

With 1:38 to go, Mahomes threw a 3-yard touchdown pass to Cameron Batson to bring his team within seven points, at 66–59. However, that was as close as the Red Raiders would get. They didn't get the ball back after that and lost the shoot-out.

The result wasn't what Mahomes had hoped for, but he did achieve his goal of delivering a standout individual performance. The quarterback battle between Mahomes and Mayfield on that Saturday evening in Lubbock is still talked about years later. Mahomes set a major-college record with 819 total yards, while his 734

"That night, those two did it as good as you could ever do it in college. I've never seen two guys do it better on the same field."[2]

— Texas Tech coach Kliff Kingsbury on the night Mahomes and Mayfield squared off in Lubbock

passing yards tied the national record. Mayfield threw for 545 yards and seven touchdowns. In total, the teams managed to break seven national records, including most total yards in a game with 1,708.

Even more amazing was the fact that Mahomes played the game with a separated shoulder. He suffered the injury three weeks earlier and had been limited in practice leading up to the Oklahoma game. Then during that game

Mahomes escapes a tackle as he scrambles for yards against TCU.

he broke his left wrist, an injury he played with for the rest of the season.

BOUNCING BACK

The following week, Mahomes and Texas Tech faced off against in-state rival TCU. This one didn't start as well for Mahomes. He turned the ball over twice in the first quarter, once on a fumble and the other on an interception. But shortly after, he turned things around. With defenders chasing him around the backfield, Mahomes fired a throw on the run to receiver Reginald Davis, who caught the ball in stride for a 33-yard touchdown.

With two minutes left in the fourth quarter, the Red Raiders trailed 17–10. Mahomes and the offense had driven into the TCU red zone. Then, on second and goal, he hit Dylan Cantrell for an 8-yard touchdown pass to send the game into overtime.

Texas Tech got the ball first. Facing second down and 10 at the 15-yard line, Mahomes looked for a receiver. Then he took off running. Avoiding contact with the defenders, the quarterback scampered into the end zone for a touchdown. TCU tied the game, but Texas Tech won it with a field goal in the second overtime. The 27–24 win had stopped a three-game losing streak. But it turned out to

SLEW OF AWARDS

After leading all of college football with 421 passing yards per game in 2016, Mahomes became a household name for many college football fans. His success also earned him a number of accolades. He was awarded the Sammy Baugh Trophy as the top college football passer. He was the fourth quarterback in Texas Tech history to win the award. In addition, Mahomes was named the Big 12 Scholar-Athlete of the Year and an Academic All-American.

be the team's only victory in a seven-game stretch that derailed its season.

The season ended with a game against Baylor at AT&T Stadium. Trailing 7–0, Mahomes led the Red Raiders' offense onto the field. Less than five minutes later, Mahomes lofted a pass 35 yards to wide receiver Keke Coutee, who came down with it in the end zone for the score.

Texas Tech and Mahomes were rolling. He found Cantrell for a 40-yard score. He connected with Quan Shorts for an 81-yard touchdown. Finally, with the ball at his 20-yard line, Mahomes threw a pass to Coutee at midfield. After breaking one tackle, Coutee sprinted for a touchdown. It was Mahomes's fourth touchdown pass of the game—and they were only midway through the second quarter.

Mahomes threw two more touchdown passes as Texas Tech finished the season on a high note with a 54–35 win. His 586 passing yards helped him become only the third college football player to post multiple seasons with more than 5,000 total yards. Those numbers came despite injuries

"We're going to score. Just give me the ball last."[3]
— Mahomes's motto while quarterbacking Texas Tech

to his left wrist and his throwing shoulder. However, at 5–7, the Red Raiders were not selected for a bowl game, so their season was over.

Fans were eager to learn whether Mahomes would be back. The quarterback made them wait and held off on announcing his decision. Finally, on January 3, 2017, Mahomes said he was going to skip his senior season and declared himself eligible for the NFL Draft. He finished his college career with more than 11,000 passing yards and 93 touchdowns.

Though the Red Raiders made only one bowl game during his career, Mahomes led one of college football's highest-scoring offenses. His next challenge would be finding success at the professional level.

A FITTING FINALE

For Mahomes, declaring for the NFL Draft was a tough decision. He had enjoyed his time with Texas Tech. But finally, Mahomes and the school released a statement announcing Mahomes's decision to turn pro.

"I know this program, with the people we've brought in and the plan we've put in place, there's a really good chance to make a run at the Big 12 in this next season and the near future," Mahomes said. "It was a really hard decision for me, but it's always been a dream to play professional sports, and the dream of going through college and wanting to be an NFL player is always what drove me."[4]

ON THE
RISE

O nce Mahomes announced he was heading to the NFL, he had less than five months to get ready for one of the biggest moments of his football career: the draft. He had a workout plan to make sure he was in the best shape possible. He also planned on meeting with NFL teams to show them he could make it at the highest level.

Mahomes received praise from national media from the moment he announced his decision to turn pro. ESPN draft analyst Mel Kiper Jr. had Mahomes ranked as the second-best quarterback available in the draft.[1] Pro Football Focus, a website devoted to analyzing and scouting football players, called Mahomes "a high risk/high reward" player.[2] The site praised Mahomes for his strong arm and his ability to avoid getting hit. It also said he had an accurate throwing arm. However, the site

Mahomes runs the 40-yard dash at the 2017 NFL Scouting Combine.

criticized the quarterback for poor footwork and making bad decisions on the field.

The first major test for Mahomes was the NFL Scouting Combine in Indianapolis, Indiana. This is a multiday event during which NFL teams can evaluate top draft prospects. Hundreds of players go through drills, tests, and interviews. The combine plays an important role in many teams' draft decisions.

Officials at the combine measured Mahomes's height and weight, along with his speed and jumping abilities. He measured in at six feet two inches (1.9 m) and 225 pounds (102 kg). Several scouts were reportedly impressed by his speed and strength. Mahomes showed off that speed in drills such as the 40-yard dash. He also took part in throwing drills.

Following the combine, Mahomes joined other former Red Raiders at the school's "pro day." Representatives from 28 of the 32 NFL teams showed up in Lubbock to watch Mahomes and his draft-eligible

FAST PASS

After passing for more than 11,000 yards at Texas Tech, Mahomes had plenty of experience throwing the ball. Many experts considered him to have the best arm of any quarterback who was eligible to be drafted in 2017. Mahomes put that arm on display at the NFL Scouting Combine in February. When throwing in front of hundreds of coaches, scouts, and team executives, Mahomes threw a pass that went 60 miles per hour (97 kmh) through the air.[3] Only two other quarterbacks were believed to have ever done that before.

Mahomes impressed the scouts with his arm strength at the Texas Tech pro day in March 2017.

teammates go through more drills. During one part of the workout, Mahomes threw a ball from his own 22-yard line to the opposite end zone, 78 yards away.[4] That was three yards longer than the longest throw of the 2016 NFL season, which went 75 yards.

Then came the individual workouts. Many NFL teams invite players to their facilities for private sessions.

Mahomes spent time with some of the NFL's biggest names, including New Orleans Saints head coach Sean Payton. Mahomes had 15 visits or workouts with teams.[5]

DRAFT DAY

After all of the workouts, the first day of the draft finally arrived on April 27. By then the teams had had plenty of opportunities to evaluate Mahomes. So did the many draft experts who work in the media. The consensus opinion was that Mahomes would be selected in the first round, which was held Thursday night. The NFL invites some of the players expected to be taken early to attend the draft, which that year was in Philadelphia, Pennsylvania. But Mahomes chose to watch the draft on TV with friends and family in his hometown of Tyler, Texas.

"He handled all the traveling beautifully and really impressed teams."[6]
— Leigh Steinberg, Mahomes's agent

They didn't have to wait long to see a quarterback selected, as the Chicago Bears selected Mitchell Trubisky with the second overall pick. Seven more teams passed on Mahomes. Then, a trade was announced between the Kansas City Chiefs and Buffalo Bills. The Chiefs had the twenty-seventh pick in the first round that year. The Bills owned the tenth pick. In order to swap positions, Kansas City gave Buffalo its third-round pick that year and its first-round pick the next year. That was a big price. It was clear the Chiefs had targeted a player they really wanted on their team.

Then Mahomes's phone rang. The Chiefs were calling to let Mahomes know they were selecting him with that tenth pick. His mother, Randi Martin, embraced her son while his agent, Leigh Steinberg, pumped his fist with excitement. His other friends and family cheered as the pick was announced live on TV.

Mahomes was the second quarterback taken in the 2017 draft and the first quarterback selected by the Chiefs in the opening round since 1983. But while the team praised Mahomes following its selection of the young quarterback, Mahomes wasn't heading to Kansas City as the team's starter. The Chiefs already had veteran Alex Smith. He had led Kansas City to the playoffs three of the four previous seasons. That meant Mahomes would begin his career as the team's backup. Unlike in college, this meant Mahomes would have some time to adapt to the new league before being forced into action. And during that time he could learn from Smith, a former first-overall pick who was entering his thirteenth NFL season.

Flanked by his mother, Randi, left, and agent, Leigh Steinberg, Mahomes gets the call notifying him that he'd been drafted by Kansas City.

WELCOME TO KANSAS CITY

Pro football is a business. Teammates aren't always friends, and in many cases they are competing for the same spot. Smith knew that Mahomes was drafted to someday replace him. Instead of being threatened by the rookie, however, Smith decided to mentor him. Shortly after the Chiefs announced they were taking Mahomes, Smith called the first-round pick to make sure there was no tension between the two players.

As the 2017 season approached, the quarterbacks spent a lot of time together. Smith invited Mahomes to lift weights with him. They watched game tapes together. All the while, Smith gave Mahomes tips for how to succeed as a pro quarterback.

The preseason offered Mahomes an opportunity for his first NFL game action. In the third quarter of the Chiefs' preseason opener against the San Francisco 49ers, Mahomes led Kansas City near the end zone. He dropped back to pass on the next play. As he avoided defenders, Mahomes floated a pass into the end zone. The receiver leaped up and caught the ball. It was Mahomes's first touchdown pass in an NFL uniform.

Throughout the regular season, Mahomes stayed mostly on the Chiefs' sideline as the backup. He looked on as Smith led the Chiefs to a 9–6 record. Heading into the last weekend

HISTORIC DRAFT PICK

When the Chiefs took Mahomes with the tenth pick in the NFL Draft, it was a historic selection for Kansas City. It was the first time the Chiefs used their first-round pick on a quarterback since they selected Todd Blackledge from Penn State University in 1983. When Mahomes helped Kansas City defeat the Denver Broncos in the 2017 regular-season finale, it was the first time a quarterback drafted by the Chiefs—in any round—had won a game for them since Blackledge did in 1987.

WORKING WITH ANOTHER PRO

Alex Smith wasn't the only veteran quarterback to mentor Mahomes in 2017. During training camp, Chiefs coach Andy Reid brought in former NFL quarterback Michael Vick to work with Mahomes. Vick played for Reid when he was the coach of the Philadelphia Eagles. During their time together, Vick helped Mahomes learn Reid's offensive style and practice using his mobility to his advantage.

of the season, Kansas City had clinched its playoff spot. The result of the finale couldn't change the team's playoff seed. Because of this, the Chiefs elected to rest Smith against the Denver Broncos. That meant Mahomes was about to get his first NFL start.

FIRST ACTION

On a cold day in Denver, Mahomes led the Chiefs' offense onto the field. Starting deep in his own territory, Mahomes dropped back to pass. His offensive line gave him plenty of time to find an open receiver. Finally he launched a pass 20 yards down the field. The ball zipped past a Denver defender before Chiefs tight end Demetrius Harris stuck his hands in the air and brought it in. This made Mahomes's first completion in a regular-season game.

The Chiefs held a 24–10 lead in the fourth quarter. At that point Mahomes was taken out of the game and

Veteran quarterback Alex Smith, left, went out of his way to mentor Mahomes during the 2017 season.

third-string quarterback Tyler Bray came in to finish things off. However, Denver responded with a pair of touchdowns to tie the game at 24–24 with 2:53 left, so Coach Andy Reid called on Mahomes to go back in.

With two minutes remaining, Mahomes rushed his team to the line of scrimmage before each play. He zipped the ball to different receivers and slowly worked the team closer to a spot where kicker Harrison Butker could attempt a game-winning field goal. The Chiefs got all the way to the Denver 12-yard line. That was close enough for Butker, who nailed the kick as Mahomes won his first NFL start, 27–24.

The next week, Mahomes returned to the bench as Kansas City played in the opening round of the playoffs. He watched as the Chiefs lost 22–21 to the Tennessee Titans. Mahomes finished his rookie season having seen limited action. In total, he had thrown

A GOOD SCOUT

Though backup quarterbacks aren't usually on the field, they have important roles behind the scenes. One of those is being part of the scout team. This is where the backup offensive players practice against the starting defense using the upcoming opponent's offensive alignment and strategy. This gives the defense a better idea of what to expect from the opponent on game day. Mahomes served the role of scout team quarterback in 2017, and he gave an early indication that he would do well when given the chance to play in games. Chiefs cornerback Darrelle Revis said that as the scout team quarterback, Mahomes would frequently "shred" the Kansas City starting defense in practice.[7]

Mahomes unloads a pass against the Denver Broncos in his first professional start.

for 284 yards and no touchdowns in one game played. The Chiefs, however, had seen enough.

On January 30, news broke that the Chiefs had agreed to trade Smith to the Washington Redskins. The move was huge news across the NFL. It was not only a big name being traded but a signal that Mahomes would begin his time as Kansas City's starting quarterback in 2018.

TIME TO
SHINE

When Mahomes showed up for the Chiefs' first minicamp in April 2018, everything had changed. He was no longer the scout team quarterback. Now everyone was looking to him to lead a team that had reached the playoffs in each of the past three seasons. Fans were anxious to see the Chiefs do more than make the playoffs in 2018.

In the months leading up to the regular season, fans and media members watched Mahomes closely. They analyzed his every move. The scrutiny picked up even more when training camp began. Fans fretted as Mahomes threw interceptions in practice. But other things Mahomes did inspired hope. During one practice, he threw a pass that traveled more than 40 yards, landing in the hands of wide receiver Sammy Watkins. Mahomes made it look effortless.

Mahomes embraced his role as a new team leader in 2018 when the Chiefs opened their training camp.

Fans were eager to see Mahomes in game action. They got that opportunity when the preseason began on August 9. Like most starting quarterbacks, Mahomes played only the first quarter of the game. He racked up 33 yards on five completions. As the preseason went on, however, fans got more glimpses of what was to come.

In Kansas City's second preseason game, Mahomes played the entire first half against the Falcons at Atlanta. With 28 seconds left in the second quarter, Mahomes dropped back to pass from his own 31-yard line. He launched a pass all the way down the field to wide receiver Tyreek Hill, who waited for it at the opposing 3-yard line. Hill made the catch and scampered into the end zone. The pass traveled 69 yards in the air—one source cited it as the longest touchdown pass in the NFL since 2000.[1]

SETTING RECORDS

Once the preseason wrapped up, the focus turned to the regular season. With skilled position players such as Hill, running back Kareem Hunt, and tight end Travis Kelce, Mahomes had the weapons he needed to excel

Mahomes prepares to throw a long pass against the Atlanta Falcons in their 2018 preseason game.

Getting solid protection from his offensive linemen, Mahomes delivers a touchdown strike to Travis Kelce against the Steelers.

from the start. But there were concerns about the Chiefs' defense and its ability to stop the run. The experts were divided on their views about the Chiefs' chances in 2018. Some analysts thought Kansas City would return to the postseason. Others predicted the Chiefs would finish under .500 and miss the playoffs.

Mahomes's first start came on the road against the Los Angeles Chargers. As division rivals, the Chargers usually play the Chiefs tough, but they were no match for Mahomes's four touchdown passes. As big as that win was, however, the Chiefs had an even greater test in Week 2. This time they were back on the road to play the Pittsburgh Steelers. Few defenses had been as consistently competitive as the Steelers' over the years. Yet once again, Mahomes and the Chiefs got the better of their opponent.

For the second straight game, the Chiefs' special teams had an early impact. Around one minute after the game started, De'Anthony Thomas returned a punt inside the Steelers' 20-yard line. A few plays later, Mahomes dropped back to pass. With time to throw, thanks to good blocking, Mahomes zipped a quick pass to wide receiver Chris Conley in the end zone. Conley brought in the pass while making sure he got two feet down inbounds. The 15-yard touchdown gave the Chiefs a 7–0 lead and quieted the raucous Steeler crowd.

On their next drive, Mahomes hit Kelce on the run. The Chiefs' tight end rumbled his way into the end zone from

19 yards out to make it 14–0. By the time the first quarter was completed, Mahomes had three touchdown passes and Kansas City led 21–0.

The Steelers weren't the type of team to roll over, though. They came back to tie the game at 21–21 in the second quarter. But they had more work to do if they were going to keep up with Mahomes and the Chiefs.

Kansas City got the ball to start the second half. A short pass to Hill netted 36 yards. Then Mahomes hit Kelce for 13 more. Finally, Mahomes found Kelce again for a 25-yard touchdown pass. Later in the quarter, Mahomes added his fifth touchdown pass of the day. Still, the Steelers once again came back to match the Chiefs' score. So once again the Chiefs' offense took the field, and once again Mahomes threw a touchdown pass. Starting from the Pittsburgh 29-yard line, Mahomes hit a wide-open Hill inside the 5-yard line. Then Hill scampered into the end zone. That turned out to be the game-winning score as Kansas City won a 42–37 shoot-out.

A HOME FIELD ADVANTAGE

Patrick Mahomes did not make a start at home for the Kansas City Chiefs until Week 3 in 2018. In the win over the San Francisco 49ers, Mahomes finally got to experience what it was like to play in front of the raucous Chiefs fans. They hold the Guinness World Record for loudest crowd roar at a sports stadium at 142.2 decibels. That's louder than a jet airplane flying 100 feet (30 m) overhead.[2]

Mahomes was off to a 2–0 start in his first season in charge.

What really caught people's attention, though, was the fact that Mahomes had thrown 10 touchdown passes in the first two weeks. That was the first time in league history a quarterback had done that. And Mahomes's six touchdown passes against Pittsburgh that September were the most for a Chiefs quarterback since Hall of Famer Len Dawson threw six against the Denver Broncos on November 1, 1964.

WELCOME HOME

The Chiefs finally made their 2018 debut at Arrowhead Stadium in Week 3, when they hosted the San Francisco 49ers. Now the home fans got to witness their new quarterback's passing feats.

With the Chiefs leading 14–7 in the second quarter, Mahomes dropped back to pass inside the 49ers' 10-yard line. He ran to the opposite side of the field

LEFT-HANDED MIRACLE

Mahomes made impressive throw after impressive throw in 2018. One of the most amazing came in the fourth game of the season. In the midst of leading Kansas City to a comeback win at Denver, Mahomes scrambled around the pocket on a second-down play. With a Broncos defender charging at him from the right, he deftly switched the ball to his left hand to avoid a turnover. Then, he flipped a pass with his nonthrowing arm to Tyreek Hill, who caught the ball and ran out-of-bounds for a first down.

to avoid the pass rush. With a split second left before a 49ers lineman got to him, Mahomes threw a strike to Conley for a touchdown. It was a perfect example of Mahomes's ability to be elusive and avoid pressure from defensive linemen. He finished the day with 314 passing yards and three touchdown passes as the Chiefs won 38–27.

The next week, the Chiefs hit the road again to face Denver. Kansas City trailed 23–13 early in the fourth quarter, but Mahomes led a late comeback that kept the Chiefs undefeated. After another win back home against Jacksonville, Mahomes and Kansas City were 5–0 to start 2018 and headed on the road to take on the New England Patriots. This would be their biggest test yet.

While the Chiefs had an exciting young quarterback in Mahomes, the Patriots had 41-year-old Tom Brady, whom many consider to be the best quarterback ever. The Patriots' starter since 2001, Brady had led the team to five Super Bowl wins. Beating Brady and the Patriots was always tough, especially on their home field in Foxborough, Massachusetts.

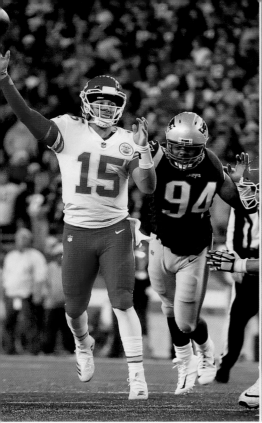

Mahomes and Hill connected seven times for 142 yards and three touchdowns against the Patriots.

In front of a national audience on *Sunday Night Football*, Mahomes and Brady entertained fans with a high-scoring affair. Though Mahomes threw a pair of interceptions in the first half, he regrouped in the second half. Kansas City trailed 40–33 with just over three minutes remaining in the fourth quarter. From his own 25-yard line, Mahomes found a wide-open Hill inside the New England 40. The speedy wide receiver raced down the sideline and outran the New England defense for his third touchdown

A QUARTERBACK DUEL

When the Chiefs faced off against the Rams, in many ways Mahomes was facing a mirror image on the opposite sideline. Like Mahomes, Rams quarterback Jared Goff had a breakout season as a second-year player in 2017. Also, Goff left the University of California–Berkeley after the 2015 season, giving up his senior year of eligibility. His replacement at Cal was Davis Webb, who transferred to Berkeley after Mahomes beat him out as the starter at Texas Tech in 2015.

of the night, tying the game 40–40. It was Mahomes's fourth touchdown pass of the game. Unfortunately for Mahomes, it was the last time he touched the ball in the game. New England got the ball back, drove deep into Kansas City territory, and kicked a game-winning 28-yard field goal as time ran out. The 43–40 loss was Kansas City's first defeat with Mahomes as quarterback.

MONDAY NIGHT MADNESS

Over the next four games, Mahomes threw 13 more touchdown passes and the Chiefs went 4–0 to run their record to 9–1. Then came their next big test, a *Monday Night Football* game against the Rams in Los Angeles. The teams came in with matching records, both sitting at the top of their respective conferences. They each had one of the NFL's most potent offenses, too.

Fans hoping for a high-scoring shoot-out got exactly what they were looking for. The teams traded score

Mahomes couldn't stop Rams linebacker Samson Ebukam from returning an interception for a touchdown during their wild game in Los Angeles.

after score. Through three quarters, the lead changed six times. Mahomes finished the game with a season-high 478 yards and six more touchdown passes. His final touchdown of the evening was a 10-yard strike to Conley to put Kansas City ahead 51–47 with just under three minutes to play. However, the Rams scored again to win 54–51.

Although Mahomes dazzled with his second six-touchdown game, the young quarterback threw a pair of interceptions in the final 1:18 to cost his team a chance at winning the game. Still, the game was historic as it was the first time two NFL teams had each scored 50 points in one game.

"He rolls around, runs around, makes plays. He has a big arm. He's talented. Plays with a great swagger. He's fun to watch."[6]

—Green Bay Packers quarterback Aaron Rodgers on Mahomes

"It was a crazy, crazy game," Mahomes said. "All that offense, and both defenses made plays that were huge momentum-changers. I basically gave them 21 points— and you can't do that against a great team like that, or you'll pay."[4]

Though it was just one game, many believed it showed that offense, not defense, was officially king in the NFL. ESPN analyst Booger McFarland declared after the game that this was the "new NFL," with Mahomes at the forefront.[5]

At 9–2, and with both losses coming against the league's best teams, the Chiefs still looked like a true contender. Mahomes, with his ability to elude defenders and find receivers all over the field, had emerged as one of the league's brightest stars. However, shortly after the Rams game, a video surfaced of Kansas City running back Kareem Hunt assaulting a woman during the previous off-season. The Chiefs released Hunt before the next game. Losing Hunt, who had already scored 14 touchdowns that season and was the NFL's leading rusher in 2017, put more pressure on Mahomes and the rest of the offense.

They responded to the setback in style. In the Chiefs' first game without Hunt, Mahomes threw four touchdown passes in a road win over the Oakland Raiders. One week later, he took the field in the fourth quarter trailing the Baltimore Ravens 24–17. In the midst of a long Chiefs drive, Mahomes went back to pass. While he was looking at the middle of the field, he threw the ball to wide receiver

INKED UP

It didn't take long for Chiefs fans to get excited about Mahomes. By the midway point of the season, fans were already getting Mahomes-related tattoos. One fan had Mahomes's face tattooed on his calf.

"Everybody wants a tattoo of the next Tom Brady," said Jeremy Taylor, the owner of the tattoo shop that executed the odd request. "Everybody's going nuts over this kid. I guess it's just because he's a winner."[7]

Demarcus Robinson, who was standing on the left side of the field. The no-look pass resulted in a first down. Analysts highlighted the play as just another example of Mahomes's versatility and ability to make throws most other quarterbacks wouldn't even attempt. The Chiefs went on to win 27–24 in overtime.

Though the Chiefs lost two of their last three games, it hardly mattered. Kansas City finished that December with a 12–4 record, clinching the top seed in the American Football Conference (AFC). Much of the attention went to Mahomes. He threw for more than 5,000 yards and 50 touchdowns, with only 12 interceptions. Those statistics alone made him the favorite to win the NFL's Most Valuable Player (MVP) Award.

When the regular season ended, however, Chiefs fans were worried about what was to come next. The team had won just one playoff game since the 1993 season, and with a shaky defense, many feared they might be vulnerable once again.

Kelce (87) had a career year in 2018 with Mahomes at quarterback, catching 103 passes for 1,336 yards and 10 touchdowns.

BREAKING
THROUGH

W hen the AFC playoffs began, Mahomes and the Chiefs found themselves sitting at home. With a 12–4 record, the Chiefs had earned a first-round bye and home field advantage throughout the playoffs. The New England Patriots were the other AFC team to earn a bye. In the wild card round, the Indianapolis Colts upset the Houston Texans. That set up a matchup between the Colts and Chiefs at Arrowhead Stadium on January 12.

After the Chiefs' special season, fans were optimistic about the playoffs. But the team's defense and history of playoff woes left some fans nervous. Kansas City had just one Super Bowl championship in its history, and that happened in January 1970. Going into the Colts game, the Chiefs had not won a home playoff game since January 1994.

Mahomes celebrates a touchdown pass during the Chiefs' playoff game against the Indianapolis Colts.

A BEST SELLER

In his first season as the Chiefs' starting quarterback, Mahomes was quickly one of the fan favorites. Through the first two months of the 2018 season, he had one of the highest-selling NFL jerseys, behind only Khalil Mack of the Chicago Bears.

Fans had reason to be concerned. Though Indianapolis was the lowest seed of the six AFL playoff teams, the Colts were on a roll. They also had their own star quarterback in Andrew Luck. The weather didn't help, either. On the day of the game, a snowstorm hit Kansas City. When Mahomes and the Chiefs ran onto the field, they were surrounded by snow. A wet field and temperatures hovering around 30 degrees Fahrenheit (−1°C) might slow the Chiefs' high-flying offense.

CHILLY CHALLENGE

The Chiefs passed their first test, stopping the Colts from getting a first down on the first possession. Following a punt, Mahomes got his first crack at postseason football. On his first play, Mahomes received the snap and faked a handoff. Then he immediately zipped a pass over the middle. The ball hit receiver Tyreek Hill in the chest. He kept moving and ran for a first down.

Later in that drive, running back Damien Williams faked out one defender and then high-stepped into the

Mahomes wasn't about to let a little snow slow him down against the Colts.

end zone for a touchdown. With just five minutes off the clock, Kansas City was already up 7–0.

Later in the quarter, Mahomes and the Chiefs were facing a third down. Mahomes rolled out to his right.

He turned his head toward the center of the field. With a defender closing in on him, Mahomes jumped and slung a pass over the middle. Hill caught it and ran forward for a first down. A few plays later, Hill took a handoff 36 yards for a touchdown to make it 14–0. In the second quarter, the Colts blocked a Kansas City punt and recovered it for a touchdown. The Chiefs now led 17–7.

Now it was Mahomes's turn to get into the action again, as he led the team deep into Indianapolis territory. He rolled out to his right. With defenders chasing him, Mahomes ran toward the right side of the field. As he approached the goal line, he reached out and put the ball over the pylon marking the front corner of the end zone for a touchdown. Kansas City now led 24–7 with the game approaching halftime. The young quarterback was living up to the hype.

With a commanding lead, the Chiefs' defense held up and allowed just one touchdown. Meanwhile, the offense held on to the ball and matched Indianapolis's score with Darrel Williams running in a touchdown from six yards out.

Kansas City went on to win 31–13. For the first time since the 1993 season, the Chiefs had won a home playoff game and were set to play in the AFC Championship Game. They were now one win away from the Super Bowl.

"We're such a different team," Mahomes said after the game. "We have such young players. We have such confidence we're going to win every game."[1]

BATTLING BRADY

One day later, the Patriots knocked off the Los Angeles Chargers. This set up a rematch of the intense Week 6 game in New England, but this time the teams would meet on the Chiefs' home turf in Kansas City. The epic matchup captured the attention of the national media. On one side, quarterback Tom Brady was playing in his thirty-ninth career postseason game. Behind Brady, the Patriots had played in the previous seven AFC title games and were looking to win their third in a row. Kansas City, meanwhile, was the upstart, with Mahomes playing in just his second playoff game.

BRAVING THE COLD

As a kid who played high school and college football in Texas, Patrick Mahomes had to make adjustments when he headed north to Kansas City. It snowed in the playoff game against Indianapolis. Then the temperature dipped below 20 degrees Fahrenheit (−7°C) in the AFC Championship Game. But Mahomes wasn't deterred by the cold.

"You've really just got to get out there and throw the ball," he said in a radio interview during the playoffs. "That's all it is. If you throw spirals and you have the right fundamentals, the ball will cut through the wind and it will cut through the cold. It doesn't matter where you're at; as long as you're throwing the ball the right way, you should still be able to do the same things whether it's 70 and sunny or zero degrees outside."[2]

The New England defense kept Mahomes bottled up throughout the first half of the AFC Championship Game.

New England made the first move in that January game, taking a 7–0 lead. Mahomes spent much of the first quarter on the bench watching the Patriots' offense.

When he came into the game, the young quarterback struggled to find his groove. It was exactly what the Patriots wanted to do—keep the ball out of Mahomes's hand. The Chiefs trailed 14–0 at halftime.

Mahomes and the Chiefs got the ball to open the second half. Just a few plays into the drive, Kansas City was facing third down. Mahomes shuffled his feet backward and looked down the field. He launched a pass to Watkins, who brought it in at the New England 12-yard line.

On the next play, Mahomes stood tall at the center of the field. Upon receiving the snap, he threw quickly to tight end Travis Kelce, who caught the ball in stride and fell into the end zone as he was being tackled. The touchdown drive took just over two minutes. Kansas City cut the Patriots' lead to 14–7.

A field goal extended the Patriots' lead back to 10 points before Mahomes got on a roll again. Starting from their own 25, Mahomes began leading the Chiefs down the field. Eight plays later, the Chiefs had reached the Patriots' 14-yard line. On the first play of the fourth quarter, Mahomes took the snap. As he ran away from a New England defender, he lofted a pass to Kelce. The sure-handed tight end dropped the ball. But there was a flag on the play. The Patriots were called for pass interference. Kansas City was awarded the ball at the 1-yard line.

On the next play, Mahomes sprinted to his right. He didn't have open space to run, and a defender was closely covering his primary target, Damien Williams. But Mahomes saw a small window of space and whipped the ball to Williams, who brought it in and fell over the line for a touchdown. The Chiefs now trailed 17–14 with much of the fourth quarter to play.

With just over eight minutes remaining, Brady threw an interception. The Chiefs took over on New England's 23-yard line. Throughout the game, Patriots defenders had chased after Mahomes and made the young quarterback make plays under duress. With that in mind, the Chiefs called a screen pass on second down. As defenders closed in on Mahomes, he tossed a short pass to Williams, who ran full-speed ahead with blockers in front of him. No one could catch Williams as he went 23 yards for the touchdown. Kansas City led 21–17 with 7:45 left in the quarter.

Suddenly, the offense the Chiefs were known for had caught a spark. When New England came back with a touchdown on its next drive, the Chiefs immediately answered to make it 28–24 with just over

Mahomes got creative as he rallied the Chiefs in the second half against the Patriots.

two minutes remaining. But as the Chiefs' offense found itself, the team's shaky defense lived up to its reputation, too. New England marched down the field

again for another touchdown to grab a 31–28 lead with 39 seconds left.

The Chiefs took over at their 31-yard line. They needed to move the ball into field goal territory in order to have a chance at tying the game. Mahomes began the drive with a completion to running back Spencer Ware, who scampered 21 yards to put Kansas City near midfield. On the next play, Mahomes dropped back deep in the pocket. Once his receivers got farther down the field, he stepped up. Then, he launched a throw down to wide receiver Demarcus Robinson, who brought it in at the New England 21-yard line with 23 seconds remaining. Mahomes took one shot at the end zone, but his pass was incomplete. Chiefs head coach Andy Reid sent out his kicker, Harrison Butker, who forced overtime with a 39-yard field goal. Once again Mahomes and the offense had come through, and now the game was headed to overtime tied 31–31.

The dream was alive for the Chiefs and their fans, but it soon ended with a thud. New England won the coin toss and got the ball to start overtime. Brady marched them down the field methodically against the exhausted

Mahomes led three big scoring drives in the fourth quarter.

A dejected Mahomes answers questions after the Patriots beat the Chiefs in overtime in the AFC Championship Game.

Chiefs defense. On the thirteenth play, Patriots running back Rex Burkhead ran two yards for a touchdown. The game was over before Mahomes and the offense got to touch the ball. All Mahomes could do was watch from the sideline as the Chiefs' dream season imploded with a 37–31 loss.

Two weeks later, the NFL held its season-ending awards show in conjunction with the Super Bowl. Mahomes was named the league's MVP. He was the first Chief ever to win the award and the fourth-youngest winner in NFL history. It wasn't a Super Bowl victory, but it was a good sign for Chiefs fans that the future was bright in Kansas City.

ONE MORE GAME

After losing to the Patriots, Mahomes had one more chance to take the football field during the 2018 season. The Chiefs quarterback was the starter for the AFC in the Pro Bowl in Orlando. This is the NFL's all-star game. In his first series, Mahomes hit Indianapolis Colts tight end Eric Ebron for an 18-yard touchdown. Mahomes finished with 156 passing yards and a touchdown. That number was good enough for Mahomes to be the offensive MVP of the game.

"It's just how the coin tosses, I guess you would say."[3]
— *Mahomes on not getting the ball in the overtime loss in the AFC Championship Game*

A LASTING IMPACT

As a promising young NFL quarterback, Mahomes immediately had opportunities off the field to take advantage of his fame. During his rookie season, he refused any endorsements that might be shown in the Kansas City area. He did this to maintain a good relationship with starting quarterback Alex Smith. "We talked about how the first year the goal was to integrate into the team, and the only way to do that is to pay deference to the incumbent veterans and try not to go into the situation with a high profile," Leigh Steinberg, Mahomes's agent, said.[1]

Once Smith was traded and Mahomes became the full-time starter, he became more open to endorsement deals. But Mahomes and Steinberg weighed his options carefully. They didn't want Mahomes to become overexposed so early in his career. "We're being very, very careful to allow this

Mahomes poses with the trophy he won for being named the 2018 NFL MVP.

ASTERISK COLLECTIVE

Mahomes and five other athletes and musicians partnered with Adidas and Foot Locker in 2018 on an initiative called the Asterisk Collective. Its mission is to help people from different communities with specific needs, such as improved mental health, career guidance, and opportunities for women. Mahomes's platform will focus on inspiring hospital patients.

season to proceed without his face on every billboard, without creating a situation where he throws the first interception and people are saying, 'Well, why's he on every billboard?'" Steinberg said.[2]

One of the first big endorsement deals for Mahomes came thanks to his love of ketchup. Several media outlets wrote about Mahomes's love for the condiment. He admitted to eating it with steak and on top of macaroni and cheese. Soon representatives from two major ketchup companies, Heinz and Hunt's, were reaching out to Mahomes. Eventually, he appeared in a Hunt's commercial. The commercial showed him lifting weights while squirting ketchup onto a bowl of macaroni and cheese.

By the end of the 2018 season, Mahomes had signed endorsement deals with other high-profile companies such as Adidas and Bose. He also appeared in a number of local ads in Kansas City. Chiefs fans saw commercials featuring Mahomes on a regular basis.

Another important endorsement deal was with the private airline company Airshare. Most of Mahomes's family lives in Tyler, Texas. But the family makes the trip north every week to watch the Chiefs play. As part of the endorsement deal, Airshare flies Mahomes's mother, father, brother, sister, and other family members to his games.

HELPING OTHERS

Mahomes also dedicated his time away from the field toward different charitable efforts. While in college at Texas Tech, Mahomes learned of a nonprofit organization called Team Luke. It supports school-age children who are hospitalized with severe head injuries. Prior to his rookie season, Mahomes raised $12,000 for the organization through an autograph signing near Texas Tech's campus in Lubbock.[3]

"The world is constantly changing, so I'm doing something about it and bring some love and support with bravery, courage, and action and providing access and exposure to new ideas to create a brighter future together and empower creativity for good."[4]

— Mahomes on working with Foot Locker and Adidas on the Asterisk Collective

Mahomes meets a young fan at a sponsor event during Super Bowl week.

Upon joining the Chiefs, Mahomes continued to work with Team Luke. During the 2018 season, Mahomes wore special cleats that featured the organization's name on them. Following the game, his shoes were put up for auction. All of the proceeds went to the organization.

"It's important to me to use my platform to share that message to kids around the world—that they can keep fighting and doing what they need to get back," Mahomes said.[5]

Mahomes's charitable work has often benefited people living in the Kansas City area. During a day off in 2018, he helped build houses for military veterans. In November of that year, Mahomes and Chiefs tight end Travis Kelce surprised a family in need with food, presents, and household products just as the holiday season was getting underway. Mahomes also purchased sports gear for 15 players on a youth football team in the Kansas City area.[6]

"The fans come out every single week and show passion and love for us and our team and what we're doing here," Mahomes said, "so for me, I want to be back in the community, giving back. And just be a part of it, to show the same love and passion to them."[7]

Aside from giving back to the Kansas City community, Mahomes has also made an effort to immerse himself in the city and its happenings. He spent much of the

SPECIAL JERSEY

Following his 2018 *Monday Night Football* game in Los Angeles, Patrick Mahomes auctioned off his game-worn jersey with the profits going to people affected by wildfires that had hit California that fall. The winning bidder paid $36,150 for the jersey.[8]

PUT TO MUSIC

Following Mahomes's 2018 performance on *Monday Night Football* against the Rams, popular rapper and Kansas City native Tech N9ne said he was considering writing a song called "MaHomie" in honor of the Chiefs' quarterback. Tech N9ne has also written songs about other Kansas City players, including a track called "Wheels Like Hill" that paid homage to speedy wide receiver Tyreek Hill.[10]

off-season prior to the 2018 season in Kansas City interacting with fans. He was seen at a country music concert that summer. Fans often saw Mahomes around town and took pictures with the young quarterback. He also became a regular at Q39, one of Kansas City's top barbecue restaurants.

On the field, Mahomes used his athletic ability, intelligence, and instincts to become one of the top quarterbacks in the NFL. Off the field, he won over fans and media with his humble and friendly personality. The bond between Mahomes, Chiefs fans, and Kansas City appears to be as sturdy as it is natural.

"They've treated me amazing," Mahomes said of the Chiefs fans. "They're really passionate about the Chiefs and they really love the players. They've taken me in and it's my home away from home now."[9]

Mahomes serves barbecue to fans at an event in 2017. He made it a priority to connect with Chiefs fans and the community after he was drafted by Kansas City.

TIMELINE

1995

Patrick Lavon Mahomes II is born in Tyler, Texas.

2000

Mahomes joins his father as he and the New York Mets play in the 2000 World Series.

2013

Mahomes announces he will play football and baseball at Texas Tech, beginning in the fall of 2014.

2014

June

Mahomes is selected in the thirty-seventh round of the MLB Draft by the Detroit Tigers.

November

Mahomes earns his first win as a starting quarterback for the Red Raiders as they defeat Iowa State.

2016

January

Mahomes announces he is leaving the Texas Tech baseball team so he can focus solely on football.

October

Mahomes ties the major-college record for passing yards in one game with 734.

2017

January

Mahomes announces he is forgoing his senior season with the Red Raiders and entering the NFL Draft.

February

Mahomes wows NFL coaches and scouts as he becomes the third quarterback in NFL Combine history to throw a pass 60 miles per hour (97 kmh).

April

The Kansas City Chiefs trade up to the number 10 overall pick in the NFL Draft and select Mahomes.

December

Mahomes experienced his first NFL regular-season action as he starts the final game of the season for the Chiefs and defeats the Denver Broncos 27–24.

2018

January
Kansas City announces it is trading then starting quarterback Alex Smith.

September
Mahomes starts the first game of the regular season for the Chiefs and throws for four touchdowns in a win against the Los Angeles Chargers; Mahomes throws six touchdown passes in the second game of the season and becomes the first NFL quarterback to throw 10 touchdown passes in the first two games of a season.

December
Mahomes threw for more than 5,000 yards and 50 touchdowns.

2019

January
Mahomes plays in his first postseason game and gets a 31–13 victory over the Indianapolis Colts; in a later game, Mahomes rallies the Chiefs from a 14–0 halftime deficit to take the lead, only to lose to the New England Patriots in overtime 37–31 in the AFC Championship Game.

ESSENTIAL FACTS

FULL NAME

Patrick Lavon Mahomes II

DATE OF BIRTH

September 17, 1995

PLACE OF BIRTH

Tyler, Texas

PARENTS

Pat Mahomes, Randi Martin

SIBLINGS

Jackson Mahomes, Mia Randall

EDUCATION

Texas Tech University

CAREER HIGHLIGHTS

- 2016 Sammy Baugh Trophy Winner

- 2016 Academic All-American Second Team

- Tenth overall pick in the 2017 NFL Draft

- First NFL quarterback ever to start a season with ten touchdown passes in two games

- 2018 First-Team All-Pro

- 2018 NFL MVP

CONFLICTS

Mahomes had to decide between baseball and football. During his second year at Texas Tech he finally gave up the sport his father played professionally. He was eventually chosen to play in the NFL. As a rookie in Kansas City, he sat behind veteran Alex Smith and played just one game all season.

QUOTE

"He loves the team atmosphere about it. In baseball, if he's pitching, he could take over a game. If he had his good stuff, it's a good chance he was going to win the game. . . . But football is a game where you've got to have everybody playing well to be successful. I think he loves that. I think he loves being in a locker room with that many guys, all of them pulling for the same goal."

—*Pat Mahomes Sr. on his son Patrick*

GLOSSARY

agent

A legal representative who negotiates employment and endorsement contracts for an athlete or other celebrity.

analyze

To closely study something for the purpose of explaining or interpreting it.

conference

A group of sports teams, usually from a common region, who play against each other during the regular season.

dart

To move suddenly or rapidly.

debut

A person's first appearance in a specific role.

division

A competitive category of teams grouped together.

endorsement

When a person receives money to use and talk about a specific product.

methodically

Moving in an orderly fashion.

mobility

The ability to move freely and easily.

pocket

The area behind the offensive line where a quarterback throws the majority of his passes.

raucous

Uproarious; behaving in a loud, zany way.

scamper

To run quickly.

scholarship

A gift of money for a student's school tuition or school supplies.

scout

A person whose job is to watch games and look for players to hire.

scramble

When a quarterback runs around quickly looking for a teammate to throw a pass to.

special teams

In football, the players on the field for kicking and punting plays.

ADDITIONAL RESOURCES

SELECTED BIBLIOGRAPHY

Baskin, Ben, and Andy Staples. "When Mayfield Met Mahomes." *Sports Illustrated*. 2 Nov. 2018. Web. 21 Dec. 2018.

Benoit, Andy, and Gary Gramling. "Can Mahomes Surpass Rodgers as the Most Talented QB Ever?" *Sports Illustrated*. 10 Dec. 2018. Web. 21 Dec. 2018.

Marlin, Robert. "Patrick Mahomes." *Tyler Today*. October/November 2015. Web. 21 Dec. 2018.

Wickersham, Seth. "The Radical Confidence of Patrick Mahomes." *ESPN The Magazine*. 14 Nov. 2018. Web. 21 Dec. 2018.

FURTHER READINGS

Derrick, Matt. *Patrick Mahomes: Showtime*. Chicago, IL: Triumph, 2018.

Gretz, Bob. *Tales from the Kansas City Chiefs Sideline*. New York: Sports Publishing, 2015.

ONLINE RESOURCES

Booklinks
NONFICTION NETWORK
FREE! ONLINE NONFICTION RESOURCES

To learn more about Patrick Mahomes, please visit **abdobooklinks.com** or scan this QR code. These links are routinely monitored and updated to provide the most current information available.

MORE INFORMATION

For more information on this subject, contact or visit the following organizations:

ARROWHEAD STADIUM
1 Arrowhead Dr.
Kansas City, MO 64129
816-920-9300
chiefs.com/stadium

This stadium holds more than 76,000 people and has been home to the Kansas City Chiefs since 1972. Mahomes made his first start at Arrowhead Stadium in 2018.

JONES AT&T STADIUM
2626 Mac Davis Lane
Lubbock, TX 79409
806-742-1196
texastech.com/facilities

This has been the home of the Texas Tech Red Raiders football team since 1947. Patrick Mahomes called this stadium home for three seasons. The stadium holds more than 60,000 fans.

PRO FOOTBALL HALL OF FAME
2121 George Halas Dr. NW
Canton, OH 44708
330-456-8207
profootballhof.com

This is the official Hall of Fame for professional football in the United States. Fans can learn about more than 300 members of the Hall of Fame and see historical artifacts from football history.

SOURCE NOTES

CHAPTER 1. PATIENCE REWARDED

1. Andy Benoit. "2018 NFL Predictions: Team-by-Team Records, Playoffs and Super Bowl LIII Champion." *Sports Illustrated*, 21 Aug. 2018, si.com. Accessed 28 Mar. 2019.

2. @WillBrinson. "Andy Reid finally bought the Ferrari his offense needed." *Twitter*, 9 Sept. 2018, twitter.com. Accessed 28 Mar. 2019

CHAPTER 2. FOLLOWING IN DAD'S FOOTSTEPS

1. Nicholas Talbot. "In the Spotlight: Mahomes' Childhood Prepared Him for Big Stage at Tech." *Lubbock Avalanche-Journal*, 11 Sept. 2015, lubbockonline.com. Accessed 28 Mar. 2019.

2. Patrick Reusse. "Hawkins Is a Proud Godfather for K.C.'s New QB, Patrick Mahomes." *Star Tribune*, 30 Apr. 2017, startribune.com. Accessed 28 Mar. 2019.

3. Brooke Pryor. "Before NFL, Chiefs' Patrick Mahomes Had to Win Another Starting Job . . . In High School." *Kansas City Star*, 19 Aug. 2018, kansascity.com. Accessed 28 Mar. 2019.

CHAPTER 3. A BALANCING ACT

1. "Texas Tech Could Start Freshman Quarterback Mahomes against Kansas State." *Fox Sports*, 1 Oct. 2014, foxsports.com. Accessed 28 Mar. 2019.

2. Peter Dawson. "MVP Contender Patrick Mahomes Was Once Told He Had 'No Future' in Football by . . . A-Rod?" *Fort Worth Star-Telegram*, 19 Nov. 2018, star-telegram.com. Accessed 28 Mar. 2019.

3. Sam Mellinger. "Now Starting for Kansas City: Patrick Mahomes . . . Right-Handed Pitcher?" *Kansas City Star*, 29 Dec. 2017, kansascity.com. Accessed 28 Mar. 2019.

CHAPTER 4. GAINING MOMENTUM

1. Sean Wagner-McGough. "Patrick Mahomes Endorses Kliff Kingsbury, Says Ex-Coach's 'Innovativeness' Would Translate to NFL." *CBS Sports*, 28 Nov. 2018, cbssports.com. Accessed 28 Mar. 2019.

2. Jake Trotter. "The Legend of Baker Mayfield and Patrick Mahomes' 2016 Epic." *ESPN*, 1 Nov. 2018, espn.com. Accessed 28 Mar. 2019.

3. Andrew Beaton. "The High-Scoring Shootouts That Made Patrick Mahomes the NFL's Next Star." *Wall Street Journal*, 5 Oct. 2018, wsj.com. Accessed 28 Mar. 2019.

4. Max Olson. "QB Patrick Mahomes Declares for NFL Draft." *ESPN*, 3 Jan. 2017, espn.com. Accessed 28 Mar. 2019.

CHAPTER 5. ON THE RISE

1. Jeff Legwold. "Ranking 2017 Draft's Top 100 Players." *ESPN*, 22 Apr. 2017, espn.com. Accessed 28 Mar. 2019.

2. "PFF Scouting Report: Patrick Mahomes, QB, Texas Tech." *Pro Football Focus*, 14 Mar. 2017, profootballfocus.com. Accessed 28 Mar. 2019.

3. "Patrick Mahomes QB." *Player Profile*, n.d., playerprofiler.com. Accessed 28 Mar. 2019.

4. Chase Goodbread. "Watch: Patrick Mahomes Unleashes 78-Yard Pass at Pro Day." *NFL*, 3 Apr. 2017, nfl.com. Accessed 28 Mar. 2019.

5. Tom Pelissero. "Patrick Mahomes Is NFL Draft's Ultimate QB Conundrum." *USA Today*, 26 Apr. 2017, usatoday.com. Accessed 28 Mar. 2019.

6. Jason Reid. "Kansas City Chiefs Trade Up to Draft Texas Tech Quarterback Patrick Mahomes." *Undefeated*, 28 Apr. 2017, theundefeated.com. Accessed 28 Mar. 2019.

7. "Darrelle Revis: Patrick Mahomes Used to 'Shred Our Defense' on Scout Team." *Yahoo*, 6 Dec. 2018, sports.yahoo.com. Accessed 28 Mar. 2019.

CHAPTER 6. TIME TO SHINE

1. John Breech. "Here's Why Patrick Mahomes' Absurd NFL Preseason Touchdown Pass for the Chiefs Was So Impressive." *CBS Sports*, 18 Aug. 2018, cbssports.com. Accessed 28 Mar. 2019.

2. "Kansas City Chiefs Break Seahawks' Loudest Stadium Record." *Sports Illustrated*, 29 Sept. 2014, si.com. Accessed 28 Mar. 2019.

3. Sam Mellinger. "It's Now up to Patrick Mahomes to Lead Chiefs in Their New Life without Kareem Hunt." *Kansas City Star*, 2 Dec. 2018, kansascity.com. Accessed 28 Mar. 2019.

4. Michael Silver. "Rams' Jared Goff Bests Chiefs' Patrick Mahomes in Epic Duel." *NFL*, 20 Nov. 2018, nfl.com. Accessed 28 Mar. 2019.

5. Mark Maske. "Rams-Chiefs Was 'the New NFL' in Its Most Spectacular Form Yet." *Washington Post*, 20 Nov. 2018, washingtonpost.com. Accessed 28 Mar. 2019.

6. Austin Knoblauch. "Aaron Rodgers Sees 'Young Self' in Patrick Mahomes." *NFL*, 22 Nov. 2018, nfl.com. Accessed 28 Mar. 2019.

7. Tom Keegan. "Kansas City on Fire for Patrick Mahomes and His Chiefs." *Boston Herald*, 15 Jan. 2019, bostonherald.com. Accessed 28 Mar. 2019.

CHAPTER 7. BREAKING THROUGH

1. "Luck-Led Colts Rally from 28 Down, Stun Chiefs." *ESPN*, n.d., espn.com. Accessed 28 Mar. 2019.

2. Kirk Larrabee. "Patrick Mahomes on Facing the Weather and Tom Brady." *247 Sports*, 15 Jan. 2019, 247sports.com. Accessed 28 Mar. 2019.

3. Nicole Yang. "What Patrick Mahomes Had to Say after Losing the AFC Championship." *Boston*, 21 Jan. 2019, boston.com. Accessed 28 Mar. 2019.

CHAPTER 8. A LASTING IMPACT

1. Jesse Yomtov. "Chiefs QB Patrick Mahomes Turned Down Endorsements Because He Wasn't Playing." *USA Today*, 2 June 2018, usatoday.com. Accessed 28 Mar. 2019.

2. "Patrick Mahomes Turning Down Big Endorsement Deals . . . Says Agent." *TMZ*, 26 Sept. 2018, tmz.com. Accessed 28 Mar. 2019.

3. "Patrick Mahomes Raises More Than $12,000 with Charity Autographs." *KCBD*, 18 July 2017, kcbd.com. Accessed 28 Mar. 2019.

4. Matt Conner. "Patrick Mahomes Joins Artists, Athletes to Form Asterisk Collective." *Arrow Head Addict*, n.d., arrowheadaddict.com. Accessed 28 Mar. 2019.

5. Matt McMullen. "Here's a Look at the Chiefs' Customized Footwear as Part of the 'My Cause, My Cleats' Campaign." *Chiefs*, 7 Dec. 2018, chiefs.com. Accessed 28 Mar. 2019.

6. Lynn Worthy. "Chiefs' Patrick Mahomes Surprises Youth Team at Shopping Event in Kansas." *Wichita Eagle*, 27 Nov. 2018, kansas.com. Accessed 28 Mar. 2019.

7. "Chiefs' Patrick Mahomes II Embracing Life in Kansas City." *Fox Sports*, 13 June 2018, foxsports.com. Accessed 28 Mar. 2019.

8. Charles Goldman. "NFL Auctioning Off Patrick Mahomes' Game-Worn Jersey to Benefit California Wildfire Victims." *USA Today*, 21 Nov. 2018, chiefswire. usatoday.com. Accessed 28 Mar. 2019.

9. "Chiefs' Patrick Mahomes II Embracing Life in Kansas City."

10. Charles Goldman. "Kansas City Based Rapper Tech N9ne Talks Patrick Mahomes with TMZ." *USA Today*, 23 Nov. 2018, chiefswire.usatoday.com. Accessed 28 Mar. 2019.

INDEX

ABOUT THE AUTHOR

James Monson is a sportswriter based in the Minneapolis–Saint Paul area. He has written articles that have appeared in various publications across the country. He has a degree in print/digital sports journalism.